To

Elain Miller
a beautiful &
magnificent kind

RICH POEMS

For

POOR HEARTS

Best wishes

John J

John J May

28-03-19

FOR...

All
Those
Holding
On.

DON'T let go.

P.S.

HANG ON.

Help
is
in
your
Hands.

Contents

AGE

I rage at old age
and howl at the fact
that the day of my demise
shall be my second last act.

I silently scream
at creeping decay
dreading on earth
my sad bad last day.

If there is a creator
does He die?
and if not
then, why I?

Life, precious life
in all its pain and pleasure
has meaning from birth to death
when love is our hearts treasure.

My last act is a life revealed
family and friends forever sealed
not in a box nor in the ground
in a heart full of love that's always found.

A smile from a child or a friend
shaking of hands to amend
misunderstandings although rare
hearts united because we care.

So listen to the words of this final letter
teaching truth of a life that's so much better
to practice kindness every day
goodbye sweet earth in your clay I now lay.

"It is not natural – to die"

ALCO-HELL   *(Written after seeing friends lives destroyed)*

Alcohol is my nemesis
Sometimes a lonely friend
Releases much suppression
To Bacchus I might amend.

Encourages lust-damages trust
Imagines problems disappear
Ha, they stay in life, but not the wife
Because of whiskey, wine and beer.

The danger of drink is innocence
Its poison fills the mind
Decisions no longer sensible
To consequences totally blind.

No woman or man decided
When young to invite madness
For here is seeds destruction
Its flower the fruit of sadness.

Shame is lurking in its pleasure
Broken dreams shout out to all
Its taste deceives our thinking
Nothing prepares for that fall.

There are also many times
When two is the time to halt
But weakness wins, I compromise
Lie and say, "It's not my fault."

Alcohol is both bad and good
Helps celebrate our worthy dreams
But drink too much too often
Only you hear silent screams.

With life so very hard
And endless days of worry
Is it really any wonder
To the bar we often hurry.

I cannot yield or weaken
Values are my life
Give me home and children
Precious comfort of a wife.

They know I have chosen
The priceless pearl of peace
An irrevocable decision
From alcohols release.

"We are what we say we are but it's what we do we truly are"

PURPOSE *(Written after a fabulous weekend in France 2008)*

What is it all
When all is told
The ceaseless toiling
For fame and gold.

We are only here
A few short years
Fighting and fussing
Laughter and tears.

Everything changes
Nothing can last
Live for today
Forget the past.

Moments of joy
So often rare
Seize them now
Drink them share.

For nothing compares
To "la joie de vivre"
Time marches on
Then it's time to grieve.

Live life to the full
Never waste one day
Tremble with purpose
Till the grave you lay.

"The end of life is the beginning of our loving legacy"

AWAKEN

Those who have no purpose
have joined the living dead.
Those who have no dreams
are like a corpse that has been bled.

Those who've known not love
are like the old who want their grave.
Those who have no friend
live life like a lonely slave.

Those who have no joy
are like a bride about to wed
abandoned at the altar
now lies crying in her bed.

Those who are dystopian
cannot help how they feel
the past a poisoned prison
laughter to them not real.

For these are the things
that truly matter
in a dangerous world
where innocent lives shatter.

Awaken to this moment
treasure beating flowing blood
look not back in anger
for life is all that's good.

*"I enjoy lying awake in the middle of the night, for darkness
sometimes produces light"*

A HEART WITHIN A TOWN *(Ode to 9/11)*

Explosive ignorant theology
takes root in soil of despair,
objections venomously ignored
planning to deny others air.

Violent destructive passions
West North South Middle East.
Who opened Pandora's Box?
for pain and death to feast.

We are born for kindness
love, not unexpected death,
Martyrs to oblivion
killed our right to breath.

Historical painful wrongs
no doubt cast in the mix,
confusing simple minds
bent on catastrophic fix.

The shock, screams, and smell
of burning flesh and fear,
oh god, your god please listen
bombers shed not one tear.

Are their hearts dead to love
when did they turn to ice?
can they not remember
when they were young and nice.

Who created this raging lust?
savagery beyond compare,
to cut, hurt and wound,
their own they would not dare.

Watches are not made
by designers to self-destruct,
nor man made to pray
"Allah is great, you're sucked."

Mohammed was a good man
tells us "to do good,"
then why do we have some
who shed much innocent blood.

The Koran like the Bible
written to lead us to God,
if a teacher preaches hate
those writings expose his fraud.

What is right and what is wrong
does not change with time,
to kill and maim and murder
is in God's eyes a savage crime.

There is no room on this planet
for weapons of mass destruction,
why not change, help each other
with ideas for kind production.

Children around our Earth
are not born to hate,
it's transfused through tradition
then violence is their fate.

Revenge becomes the mantra
cruelty a daily creed,
blood sacrifice their passion
then scream until they bleed.

But stop for one moment
consider God above,
is He a God of poison?
or the father of a mother's love.

Can he derive some pleasure
when his creation bombs and kills,
when his children scream in agony
adding to mankind's many ills.

New York is one great town
welcoming all races to her city,
but on the morning of 9/11
thousands were shown no pity.

Working, laughing, talking
in two huge magnificent towers,
the god of death came stalking
and would bury them in hours.

Innocence died that day
our dreams began to rust,
when steel and lives collapsed
turning everything to dust.

Shock turned to anger
as rivers of tears did flow,
and leaders of free men
wanted this world to know.

Never, no not ever
surrender to the god of sorrow,
civilised men show compassion
forever, not just tomorrow.

Never, no not ever
shall I teach a child of mine,
to hurt by word or deed
view fellowman as swine.

The future is quite uncertain
our past, shocking and quite bleak,
our earth is but a village
where all men peace should seek.

For war produces widows
and widows produce the men,
who start the madness over
and begin their wars again.

"The day we decide to truly live is the day KINDNESS becomes our religion"

LIFE

Conceived in passion
Carried with love
Born in pain
Gift from above.

Life sweet life
Mysterious so good
Joy mixed with tears
Water and blood.

Innocence destroyed
Dreams not true
Acceptance of reality
Each day new.

Health and sickness
Daily chores
Years of sameness
Heart-sick sores.

Laughter and music
Happiness in time
Stillness, contentment
Ungratefulness a crime.

Friends and lovers
Criss-cross our days
Each unique
In so many ways.

Come morning come night
Time to wonder
Our plans and schemes
Torn asunder.

Rushing pushing
Everything so fast
Is anything permanent?
Does anything last?

Mixture of motives
Trying to please
People resent
Living on their knees.

Struggle and pleasure
Excitement bursts through
One day victory
Yet, why so few?

Live it – love it
Why complain
We shall not pass
This way again.

Give life seek peace
Then surely know
The good we do
Is what we sow.

Innocent hearts
Complexities multiply
Contradictions daily
Millions cry.

Nothing is easy
Mistakes every day
Philosophers ponder
For a different way.

Yes - shouts the fool
No - cries the broken man
 Life is what you make it
And make it, we can.

Why - asks the child
How - asks the student
The poet chooses silence,
Knowing quietness is prudent.

If there is a secret
To enjoy the way we live
It must be in our nature
To share - to love - to give.

Sharing is unselfish
Loving is to grow
Giving equals kindness
Living is to know.

That life is a precious gift
Never ever to be wasted
Appreciating this simple fact
Life's joys we will have tasted.

"Life, suffused with problems, saved through love"

THE TYRANNY OF TIME

The rage of age shatters what matters
leaves young flesh cold when old
as we try to hide what wounds our pride
leaves our confidence in tatters.

Years, tears, fears accumulate with time
then steals a lovely treasure
an unlined face as we lose the race
of a life with love and pleasure.

It happened so fast, we thought it would last
we innocently believed in schemes
then life struck back with another crack
exposed our impossible dreams.

A love that dies, a soul that cries
a sore that may not heal
a cut so deep our memories keep
for hearts are not made of steel.

Trust and lust were given and lost
as soul-mates locked and bonded
words were said soft feelings bled
then lovers soon absconded.

The Rolling Stones sang with a twang
a song about freedom and time
being on our side as we ride
towards Adam's greatest crime.

It's not okay to waste one day
since life is oh so brief
and you might lose if you refuse
to oppose the graveyards thief.

Come what may that unwelcome day
throws a shadow on all our goals
it robs our youth and speaks a truth
that infects our very souls.

And if by chance we live to dance
until we are ninety-two
we will still be blue because so few
remained from when life was new.

"I have loved and lost but never lost love"

METAMORPHOSIS

Sweet sleep creeps up softly slowly
as I lie in my lonely bed
her face appears before me
I remember things she said.

I know not why it happened
how her tender heart turned to ice
still, I have great memories
which helps me live life twice.

Is there one woman alive today
anywhere on this tortured planet
who can guarantee her lover
her metamorphosis shall not be granite.

Passion fuels the soul
of many a selfish man
and the rock we always perish on
is, we do not see her plan.

No female will endure
mans ability to humiliate
the woman who loves her man
and a fool who seals his fate.

"There comes a moment in every man's wife, when she decides the man for her life"

OUR MYRIAD NATURES

We are bad and good
plus contradictory.

We are true and false
plus complex.

We are hypocritical and sincere
plus puzzled.

We are humble and proud
plus dark.

We are ignorant and knowledgeable
plus strange.

We are corrupt and innocent
plus angelic.

We are destructive and creative
plus dreamers.

We are secretive and open
plus weird.

We are violent and pacifistic
plus cowards.

We are gregarious and lonely
plus silent.

We are thinkers and dumb
plus confounded.

We are religious and pagan
plus liars.

We are sad and happy
plus bizarre.

We are young and old
plus dreamers.

We are cruel and kind
plus remorseful.

We are so much and so little
our true selves so brittle
we see with our hearts eye
that you are you, and I am I.

*"I am filled with contradictions that is a fact, I cannot be no other,
as this is how I act"*

THE VIRUS

Seeds of love sown with care
its fruit so visibly spread
roots go deep, branches strong
burns until it is dead.

Seeds of love undefiled
one only has to taste
her purity of sweetness
to eat one must make haste.

Seeds of love grow so pure
weeds are also there
action must be taken
if love we wish to share.

Seeds of love are poisoned
by deeds or words so bad
that the victim of this virus
screams "life is surely mad."

Seeds of love are everywhere
but the virus seeks to choke
pregnant fruit that's growing
until its heart is broke.

Seeds of love are desperate
Its enemy, fleshly lust
this poison sinks its fangs
and breaks the chains of trust.

Seeds of love got lost
in its place crept fear
jealousy its playmate
its cost was, oh so dear.

Seeds of love are gone
its harvest cruel and shallow
ploughing the soil of hope
its birth in spring lies fallow.

Deeds of love are lasting
small seeds can live and grow
its needs are love and care
and bleeds to really show.

Yesterday is but a shadow
today, the only time to live
tomorrow we can but hope
our love to surely give.

"Love is the only true magic"

PAGAN APOLLO *(On the death of our great poet Seamus Heaney)*

Anything Can Happen
It did, you died
Yet death silences not
Poetic words,
Digging with your pen
The bottomless pit of feelings
You unleashed sympathy
For tribal prisoners
Chained to poisonous myths
And united hearts
In our world village
Your town.

Anything Can Happen
Yes, gone with the wind
Seventy four years
Prospecting for truth
Falsely found
In orgies of belief
Melted by ink
On paper
On minds
Gold-dust lines
Tattooed on hearts.

Anything Can Happen
Awards-triumphs-failures
Jealousy, oh yes, inveterate
Your dripping syntax
Creating dreams
Demolishing miasmic falsehoods
Uncoupling fear
Strangling loneliness
Perpetuating childhood realities

Of innocence spoiled
Hurts too soon – wounded
Metaphysical metamorphosis.

Anything Can Happen
A sudden memory of mother
Our bridge to sanity
Salve for cuts to minds
Bandage for spoiled dreams
A silent tomb opens for
Our sonorous son
Not for him – pietism
Nor speeches echo of emptiness.

Here lies a man
His lapidary language
Immortal.
The poet of life.

"Growing old makes my blood run cold as I lie on my bed cogitating being dead"

TOUCHED BY LOVE   *(For my cousin Lynette May, on her beautiful marriage when she and her new loving husband knew she was dying.)*

Love is the key
Life its lock
Laughter the medicine
For realities shock.

Mornings hope's
Daytimes dream's
Evening calmness
Nights moonbeam's.

Past times present
Forged in the mind
Memories softly touched
Heartbeats blind.

Flowers in bloom
Sun in the sky
Smiles on lips
Tears in eye.

Swans serene
Butterflies prance
Child's stone on lake
The soul does dance.

Family and friends
Mingle as one
The marriage of love
Has just begun.

"To have good memories is to live twice"

LIFE-ABORTION-DEATH

Experts differ
Victims cry
Fathers plead
Women die.

The right to life
Marching towards death
Strangled before
Life's first breath.

Fully formed
Precious foetus
Moral dilemma
Expel detritus.

Egg and sperm
Grow in womb
Living graveyard
Not a tomb

The right to live
Choose for two
Solomon's wisdom
Regrets, some few.

A father's word
A mother's voice
Three lives enmeshed
Painful choice.

Dignity passion
Terror and blood,
A woman's decision
Can only be good.

She loves her flesh
Adores her child
Conscience clean
Squinting windows soiled.

Simplistic answers
Destroyer of dreams
Enmeshed in complexity
Nothing as it seems.

We live but once
Yet some die twice
Condemning women
Hearts of ice.

The prognosis is
Not wrong or right
Respect for each other
In this deathly fight.

The struggle to live
Our will to survive
Shake with purpose
Yes, I am alive.

"I know for certain that much of what I know is not certain"

(This concept is from English poet John Keats and implies the ability to see beyond our cultural, religious, political and social circumstances so we can see the universality of mankind! Hence the title.)

NEGATIVE CAPABILITY

Certainties contaminate peace
poison artistic mystery
imprison innocence
strangle Socratic freedom.

Born in shadowed purity
by beings, flawed
polluted by "blood sacrifice"
damaged cognitively.

Music, poetry, art, truth
like Y H W H
centrality of essence
tetragrammaton of life.

Tribal loyalties tattooed
on receptive hearts
minds open, to close
on mercy.

Opinions showered generationally
unquestioned unexamined unexplained
seeds of confusion
ripen in time for war.

Freedom from conflict
accepting uncertainty
Philosopher's Stone of imagination
to see our blindness.

To know, we know not
never did
never will
knowing is unknowing.

"Truth is beauty
beauty is truth"
in art, in life
in love.

Savagery of hatred, melted
in the fierce furnace
of kind humanistic empathy
our civilising medicine.

Our earth, one home
one family, disunited.
one cause, certainties
one cure, compassion.

The loneliness of living
in passionate thoughts
that separate us
from our sisters and brothers.

Thinking, not deeply
bestowed cruelty, slavery, armies
religious convictions
sincerely catastrophically vicelike.

Traditional chains
roots of violence
toxic Shamans
angels of death.

Historic wrongs
bleed into consciousness
birthing anger
beating hearts of revenge.

Who says "A man is my enemy"
when "he did me no wrong"
Who orders massive destruction?
on our innocent children.

Tears mayhem murder anxiety
infantile attempts to reconcile
broken dreams of unity
creeping opium of power.

Subconsciously we doubt
the 'rights' of our wrongs
to stain with pure blood
cavernous pit of Hades.

In sincerity we purpose
neighbours reactive
lives damaged,..... ruinously
perceptions invoked, always.

Prayers to deaf gods (except Mars)
each side knowing
their holy crusade of terror
is righteous in ice cold eyes.

Redemptive purity
lost in time, squandered
vanished in paradise
through chimerical convictions.

Purchased with blood
sanctified by tears
worshipped through memory
eulogised over coffins.

Cultural mythologies
salvational Prozac
pathetic placebo
pleasing everyone, almost.

Hidden wounds
public bravado
cultural pretension
consistent untruths.

Certainly we know
the incomprehensibility
of dramatic sudden conflict
broken friendships, families, nations.

Its seed, nebulous creeds, opinions
planted in childhood soil
harvested in the living walking dead
to perpetuate ongoing pyrrhic victories.

"Man's propensity for violence is exposed by women's proclivity for love"

MISSING

WHERE IS SHE
The woman of my dreams
solution to my schemes.

WHERE IS SHE
The other half of me
owner of life's key.

WHERE IS SHE
The meaning of my life
woman to make my wife.

WHERE IS SHE
Is she so very far away
I looked yesterday and today.

WHERE IS SHE
Why is she so hard to find
to her I would be kind.

WHERE IS SHE
My woman, my life, my reason
I search in every season.

WHERE IS SHE
My lover, my life, my friend
to find her my search would end.

WHERE IS SHE
To give meaning to my soul
complete my life, make whole.

WHERE IS SHE

"Lack of appreciation is the seed of destruction for friendship, romance, love and marriage"

MOTHER

The day my mother died
She lived
In me
Through me
For me
Her lapidary words
Chiselled on my heart
She the hammer
Me the anvil
Blood on blood.

"A mother's loving kindness is the certain seed of lasting good mental health"

THE PAST

The past has come to haunt me
like bad dreams as if awake,
searing through my psyche
oh heart, oh endless ache.

The past has stayed to live
resides within my home,
if memories are so good
then, why am I alone?

The past arrived silently
indifferent to its cost,
teaches those still mourning
the value of what was lost.

The past my daily prison
mind's eye can truly see,
choice the lying crime
never shall I be free.

The past yes lingers longer
than snow on a mountain peak,
and whispers in our ears
let reason surely speak.

The past is today's tomorrow
chained to me every hour,
Chinese drip-drip-drip of pain
taste life's love, turned so sour.

The present is our past
to each is quite unique,
tremble with one purpose
love's loss forever seek.

"Time is a great healer: it's not"

VALUES

A kind man is happy
he has learned to give,
A selfish man is sad
never knowing how to live.

A sick man is well
if he values health,
A healthy man is sick
whose only goal is wealth.

A rich man is poor
whose friends cannot be real,
A poor man is rich
whose friendships are of steel.

The man who values love
above all earthly treasures,
shall never squander happiness
for some passing shallow pleasures.

Yes, principles and values
are the arteries of the soul,
flowing freely through our hearts
cleansing thoughts to make us whole.

"The four pillars of contentment are: Acceptance-Simplicity-Kindness-Gratitude"

APHRODITE

The mystery of her innocence
caught me by surprise,
my heart beat ever faster
as I looked into her eyes.

Two strangers met one night
to each other quite unknown,
words were said, passions fed
resulting depth was sown.

Her beauty was quite obvious
then she gave a smile,
instantly I needed her
to stay with me awhile.

Her dazzling face enhanced
her sweet angelic voice,
I was now her abject prisoner
I simply had no choice.

What is this holy power
that women possess within,
that man will sell his soul for
then unrepentantly sin.

Her sensual chains capture
willing minds of mortal men,
we are her willing subjects
and want her over again.

As she spoke I realised
this Aphrodite was so rare,
her radiance so lovely
from her feet up to her hair.

This goddess of sensuality
exuded magnetic sex appeal,
so erotically and sincerely
I wondered, is this lady real.

Who is this feminine vision
what goes through her mind,
that leaves her lovers trembling
and to consequences blind.

She laughs at life's dangers
as if there is no tomorrow,
is she one of those wise ladies
knows not the pain of sorrow.

A man can live a life
in one night of sexual pleasure,
and this woman as a wife
would be her lover's treasure.

For no one knows the future
gone forever is our past,
and if I have one wish
I hope this lusting love will last.

*"Little boys worship their mothers, little men worship themselves,
but a real man will always worship the woman he has willingly
chosen as his goddess"*

TRAVESTY

Injustice hangs like Damocles sword
suspended on a slender thread,
its febrile fury sinks its blade
into flesh, whose mind has bled.

Justice prowls in human hearts
Nuremberg made its choice,
millions died, children cried
the dead now had a voice.

Who speaks for those accused
by whispering believable lies,
lives damaged by fabrication
visible in demented eyes.

What rage is this!
that screams at God in vain,
is mercy missing from our race
can no one sense the pain.

Leaders move to legislate
make laws for common good,
rules for people bad and cruel
yet innocence misunderstood.

Has justice eyes to see
the blindness of mans soul,
knowledge may not yield fairness
for it's kindness that makes us whole.

Prosecutors often seek
some non-crimes to be true,
Salem "witches" doomed
child's fingers point at you.

Nineteen innocents hanged
justice died that day,
twisted hearts triumphed
hope buried in the clay.

Tyranny rules through fear
punishes any who dare speak,
courage asks one question
"Is not truth the pearl we seek?"

Greek tragedies emphasise
gods of war and pride,
condemning mankind to sorrow
when truth they tried to hide.

Justice is the prize
balancing our golden scales,
injustice the fanged poison
that crucifies, then jails.

Hearts of granite stone exposed
through eyes not yet closed blind,
for truth and fairness always lives
in pure hearts, forever kind.

"To trust is to freeze suspicion"

WHY FRIENDSHIP DIES

Our friendship is dead
over what you said,
not what you did
or what you hid.

The day it died
was because you lied,
your words were cruel
that poured more fuel.

On lingering spite
that added bite,
to words so wrong
that could not belong.

To a heart once kind
yet now so blind,
the start of madness
whose seed was badness,
and buried in the clay
our friendship that sad day.

"We sometimes lose true friends, but rarely true enemies"

THE BEAUTY OF LOVE   *(A poem for a very sick special child)*

Hannah was perfect
the day of her birth,
one gorgeous baby
delivered on earth.

A beauty born
a babies tears,
her father's smile
her mother's fears.

A little girl
becomes a child,
in constant pain
yet always mild.

Exquisite eyes
beautiful face,
mammy clothed her
in love and lace.

She knows those
who love her most,
if Hannah could speak
her voice would boast.

I love especially mammy
and grandma too,
daddy and Brian
but, it's when I'm blue.

"I WANT MY GRANDAD
the man of my dreams,
he holds me close
he soothes my screams,

he makes me laugh
he stops me cry
looks into my eyes
and asks God, why?"

A little girl
with a heart of gold,
has carved her niche
in the family fold.

Her mind so clean
her soul so pure,
her master today
shall one day cure.

For surely if
there's God above,
his message must be
one of pure love.

And Hannah's life
teaches us today,
to never complain
and sometimes pray.

Expressions of thanks
for friends and blood,
and be like Hannah
a child oh so good.

*"There is no sorrow worse than the death of a child, and no words
of mine can alleviate that awful pain. However there are only two
possibilities; either there is a God, therefore a resurrection.
If no God no resurrection.*

A FATHERS DEATH   *(On the death of a friend's father)*

It should not happen
My god, my father, my life
As a little boy I knew
He could not die
My strength, my joy, my hero
My life, my everything.

I did not know
Your age, your dreams
I only knew your love
And I needed nothing else
You were my everything.

My hero, my friend, yes yes
I looked up to you
I admired you
I wanted to be like you
Your compliments were my nectar.

My dad, my everything
Now you're gone
I am alone
In a lonely world
But, I have your wise words.

I am now you
You live on in me
How can I thank you
I can't, not now or ever.
So I say dad – I love you.

"To lose ones parent is to almost lose ones mind, especially if they were gentle and kind"

SEVENTY FIVE   *(A Life of 27,375 Days)*

Racing Pacing Rushing Pushing
Thinking Blinking Breaking Sneaking.

Dreams Schemes
Nights Frights Rights
Sickness Happiness Hopelessness
Friends Family Lovers Fighters Dieters.

Lust Trust Worst
Sex Ex
Music Laughter Years Fears Beers
Cool Fool Rule.

Addictive Restrictive Repulsive Competitive
Passion Fashion
Alive Jive Live
Death Breath Bread Fed.

Hit Memories Poetry
Cash Hash
Pain Gain Sane Cane
Mad Bad Sad Glad Fad Dad.

Orgasm Chasm Sexism
Mask Ask Cask
Bleed Steed Deed Need
Romance Dance Chance.

There are seventy five words in my poem, meaning seventy five reasons to illustrate and illuminate the baby-boomer generation.

ESSENCE OF BEING *(I wrote this in 1973 under the name Christian De Silva)*

Man's mind knows peace – His ears war

Man's eyes see hurt – Peoples penalty

Man's hands know work – His flesh injustice

Man's feet know pain – Sweet exhaustion

Man's heart knows grief, intimately – Sorrow sadly

Man's strength knows weakness – His frailty, tears

Man's blood seeks fulfilment – His woman, his extension

Man's body knows sickness – His spirit knows not

Man's pride is vanity – Abstract hollow value

Man's power seeks challenge – Accepted, rejected, won

Man's prescience numbs – Uncertain future

Man's utilitarianism – Commercially devastated

Man's ambition knows simplicity – Elusive quality

Man's happiness grasps constancy – Diamond of existence

Man's experience teaches wisdom – Yet perennial mistakes

Man's totality bears fruit – Seed of continuity

Man's observation of man – Beclouds vision, horizon vanished

Man's pity craves explanation – Treacherous fortune, why?

Man's love seeks eternity – Self perpetuating ability

Man's fear is mortal transience – Time its food

Man's belief, truth – Fuel of his being

Man's purpose, freedom – Music and wine of health

Man's brilliance his greatness – Its produce his shame

Man's beauty rests – On dignity his pillar

Man's problems – Man made

Man's searching – Never ends

Man's knowledge – A skin scratch

Man's dreams see good – Reality laughs

Man's hope – Spark to conquer

Man's life is short lived, ravished by worry, perplexed by woe, inhibited by custom, confused by tradition, yet we triumph, through misery, elation, tragedy, excitement, our now, today, tomorrow, a creature of splendid nobility stands erect in innocent ignorant lustre, a masterpiece of umbilical ingenuity, you, me, men of old, our posterity.

HISTORY   *(I wrote this poem in the throes of discovering the joy*
of living, as it had dawned on me the secret was giving)

FIFTY YEARS AGO
You hurt me
made me cry,
what wounded most
your truthful lie.

FORTY YEARS AGO
You insulted me
never sensed my pain,
made things worse
assuming it was feign.

THIRTY YEARS AGO
You cursed me
laughed when I was cold,
if slavery was legal
I would be lost and sold.

TWENTY YEARS AGO
You danced on friendship
ruined what I held dear,
could I hold on to this
endure another year.

TEN YEARS AGO
You ignored me
I tried to reconcile,
reached out my hand
pitifully for a little while.

History is our prison
poison of the past,
redemption is in knowing
not even life can last.

Freedom from past pollutions
cleanses the living dead,
looking back in sorrow gone
like skin on a snake that's shed.

Turmoil in the mind
ceases to control
the damage others did,
now our being is whole.

What good is anger
vented on a friend,
revenge a merciless enemy
its only goal to rend.

Years passed gone
memories infect the flesh,
reminiscent of people past
always striving to enmesh.

If history is our torment
make freedom your only goal,
forgive the past and people
and live a life made whole.

"I have learned that words are permanent and cannot be unsaid;
and words that wound the heart, leave love and friendship dead"

MY LIFE

Sometimes when it's quiet
I wonder why I spend my days,
rushing here and pushing there
often in a daze.

The poet David H Thoreau once said:
"Most men lead lives of quiet desperation,"
for me, I am not sure if that's true
but what is, is daily exasperation,

at having to earn a living
fight for my loaf of bread,
but if I did not work
family would not be fed.

I'm not young or not yet old
and have come to realise,
to appreciate the gift of life
is to see it through children's eyes.

Yes I have lost my innocence
corruption seeps in every day,
disappointments multiply
threatening to turn me grey.

But I have chosen to accept
the price we all must give,
to enjoy daily co-existence
banish negativity and live.

How? By simply recognising
that life is oh so short,
of course we must experience
of course we will get hurt.

The secret lies in recognition
of one very simple fact,
that if we help our fellowman
then we simply have to act.

Philosophers rack their brains
attempting to understand,
mans appearance on this earth
and his ruining of our land.

Politicians set up systems
regulating peoples' every move,
punishing with a vengeance
anyone not in their groove.

Religious leaders perfected
centuries in the past,
inventions from godless minds
heavens and hells that last.

A mind breaks free
when a heart accepts,
that much of life's pain
is simply childhood precepts.

What is life? I have to ask
not to question is slow poison,
as the mind is denied its nurture
which is our use of reason.

I cannot live on this earth
without asking, why must I die,
there are times when life is so good
the very thought of death makes me cry.

There is no answer, there never was
I know that in my heart,
that's why we banish discussions
of the day we finally must part.

Life is not about sadness
melancholy and the rest,
oh no my friends, now hear this truth
life is about joy and happiness.

I can only speak for me
what I've experienced up to now,
and if you listen very carefully
I shall reveal the secret how.

To enjoy each day no matter
what trials we find ourselves in,
is to treasure simple pleasures
then our joy will shine within.

My existence is but a moment
in the history of time,
but squandered possibilities
now that surely is a crime.

So my determination
is to make the best of what I've got,
and written on my tombstone:
"No Regrets" when they lay me in my plot.

"kindness is the seed that produces lasting peace"

MY MOTHER

Bursting from her body
little did I realise
a mother loves her baby
especially when it cries.

My earliest memory of my mother
was her combing my brown hair
and if ever I hurt myself
she was always quickly there.

School years passed quite slowly
but I never forgot that day
when she came in to the yard
and sat and watched me play.

I did not score a goal
we did not even win
but what really made me love her
was the fact that she came in.

My mother taught me rules
respect for people's rights
fairness was her virtue
when judging my many fights.

I asked the usual questions
during puberty regarding sex
invariably her reply was
"No son, that subject is an x."

She taught me her religion
showed me how to pray to God
but during those rebellious years
I thought the whole thing was a cod.

When I fell in love she said:
"Son remember this
be truthful and unselfish
then your marriage will be bliss."

When our first baby was delivered
who was first on the scene but mother
and I knew then for certain
I would never want another.

She has never been a gossip
when there's trouble she just sighs
her tongue she can control
which makes her very wise.

If I have any concerns
she worries about them too
then she'll invite me to her house
and together we'll see them through.

The years are rushing past
as I watch my mam grow old
and the thought of her passing
makes my blood run cold.

For the children of her body
love her one and all
and if she has a problem
she can on any of us call.

She has marked her brood
with a legacy from above
she wrote it in our hearts
for one another, simply love.

How do we measure a mother's love?
there really is no way
and if we do neglect them
stop, give something back today.

She will not last forever
but I swear she will live on
for I shall teach my children
her words, from the day that they are born.

"There is no face more beautiful, no heart kinder, no voice sweeter, no words wiser than a mothers"

BOXING   (Ode to boxer Katie Taylor on winning a world title in 2012: This poem was recited on the Ryan Tubridy radio show)

Katie Taylor is an Irish boxer
of that there is no doubt
for years she trained and fought
for this final Olympic bout.

A heart of gold
and fists like steel
her punches landing
each one real.

A young lady from
a town called Bray
pulverised opponents
and won today.

A crown of victory
a medal of gold
her spirit on fire
her purpose bold.

She fought like a warrior
she won like a queen
and the Irish cheered
for what they'd just seen.

A magnificent spectacle
of talent and power
goddess of the ring
who would not cower.

She danced and punched
with furious intent
till the final bell rang
her strength now spent.

The heart of a nation
beating now as one
were wondering if
her fight was won.

Then came the result
and a nation roared
an Irish princess
had fought and scored.

Her mission accomplished
a dream come true
years of practice
but this she knew.

"Guts and stamina
blood and tears
land the blows
forgot her fears.

Forged a path
for others to follow
and live our lives
for a better tomorrow.

"A woman triumphing in a man's world is a disaster for misogynists"

FALLING IN LOVE

Nothing in life compares
to the stomach churning thrill
when two people connect and know
for this feeling they could kill.

It's coffee in the morning
sunshine all day long
it's knowing in your heart
this love cannot be wrong.

It's poison to the sceptics
nectar to our youth
it's prison for the willing
it shines in beauty's truth.

Soothes man's savage nature
peace to his troubled soul
it's one of life's few miracles
cleanses until we're whole.

Awakening of our dreams
that we all possess
it's reaching for the stars
the lover can do no less.

It's smiling first at strangers
because of that internal glow
the feeling of being loved
we need the world to know.

Never in human history
could a love have been this strong
two lives bleeding into one
two spirits singing the dreamers song.

The magic of a kiss
the music of desire
we need this love to last
until we both expire.

The thrill of willing passion
the ecstasy of gifted flesh
every single act of love
is new and good and fresh.

No matter what the future
nothing can change this fact
Cupid shot that arrow
and wounded us to act.

Life or death, peace or war
we have chosen this way to live
and each day on this planet
we seek our love to give.

Surrendered to each our freedom
mingled our sweat and blood
for loving has set us free
to fiercely choose what's good.

To each and every person
may you heed Cupid's call
for there is nothing nicer
than that lucky day we fall.

"Falling in love: A drug like no other, falling out of love: A pain like no other"

FRIENDS

One day last year I realised
friends do not come cheap
they can cause us pain and hurt
the wounded do not sleep.

Affection develops over time
expectation increases too
but the anvil of its measure
is forgiveness, then it's true.

My friends are quite varied
Individual in their taste
and to overlook their faults
is to solidify the paste.

Of talk and dreams and laughter
in their company year by year
and when trouble hits my doorstep
I know, they are always there.

How they put up with me
is something of a mystery
I guess it must be as I said
Friend's faults become mere history.

When I go out on the town
somewhere nice to meet
the magic of the night is born
with friends who are so sweet.

Over time there have been rows
some have drifted away
but once a friend decides to part
nothing can make them stay.

Misunderstandings are the source
causing friendships to decay
and when good pals lose each other
it causes anguish and dismay.

So much has been written
about keeping friendships live
yet if we are totally honest
most of us have not five.

Why I ponder, does it happen
friends are hard to make
when loneliness surrounds us
I wonder is it me, who may be fake!

Children do it every day
they make it very clear
being simple and oh so honest
friendships they do hold dear.

It gets awkward as we grow older
of that there is no doubt
sophistication starts to grow
natural friendships might not sprout.

So if you have good people
whom you know are true friends
be very careful with their feelings
and if you hurt them make amends.

To grow old alone one day
surely qualifies as sadness
not to nurture solid friendships
definitely qualifies as madness.

No matter what the problem
apologise be humble
don't risk losing something precious
for why should lasting beauty crumble.

If during life's short troubled voyage
we have hammered out one real friend
be careful not to lose that joy
treasure it to the very end.

"To find one true friend is to lose our hearts to unselfishness"

HEART-CRIMES

There are humanities crimes
Rivers of blood
Oceans of salt tears
Poison of intolerance
Invective of hatred
War

Life is tough

Heart-crimes are different

The husband who drinks;
instead of eating at home

The lover who lies;
because of the other lover

The friend who betrays;
a friends confidence

The boss who belittles;
 workers

The priest who publically shames; (likely a hypocrite)
the outward sinner

The father who breaks his promise;
to his trusting children

The parent who prefers;
one child over another

The teenager who calls names;
to the less fortunate

The mate who humiliates;
his/her mate

Lovers who pretend;
to love

The pretentious who shower sincerity;
on the gullible

The person who stands someone up;
on a date (Guilty)

All are destroyers
of innocence
and to destroy purity
is to self destruct.

To break a heart
is to inflict
a wound
that takes years
to heal
if ever.

A kind soul
needs
no moral police
because
their fuel
is gentleness
and gentle souls
rarely commit
crimes against
fellow creatures.

"Repent"

DUBLIN MY DUBLIN

Awash with laughter
Pain and pleasure
Adrift in progress
Change and leisure.
DUBLIN MY DUBLIN

Cursed and blessed
Sweat, struggle and beers
The city I treasure
A town full of tears.
DUBLIN MY DUBLIN

Heartbreak and victory
Poverty and wealth
Tenements and mansions
Dreams caught by stealth.
DUBLIN MY DUBLIN

Emigration cursed and seared our soul
Generations took that poxy dole
Tenements closed, suburbs took root
Education began to produce her fruit.
DUBLIN MY DUBLIN

Writers and poets born in blood
Musicians and thinkers said what they should
Conform or be-jaysus in exile you'll rot
'No-never' wrote our dreamers
'We would rather be shot.'
DUBLIN MY DUBLIN

"When I was a poor boy living in a poor city, I never realised just how rich I was"

BLIND DATE

Why did I agree
I am embarrassed.

The word is
She is beautiful
What if she is
And doesn't like me.

What if she's ugly
And does!

What will I say
Am I mad
Who knows
Who cares
Two people
Lives apart
Maybe interlocked
Good vibes
Mysterious ingredients
Pretension.

Try
Why not
Why
Need
Excitement
Date the blind.

"If the blind lead the blind both might fall in love"

LOOKING FORWARD BACK

Let us drink to the joy of wine

Fond memories of life's loves lost

Dance and sing for what's now mine

Praise melts times creeping frost

"It is better to have loved and lost; than own a heart, ice cold in frost"

MEMORIES

The ecstasy of solitude
imprisons memories of my past
and if life is for laughter
then live to make them last.

The absurdity of conflict
madness of even one lost day
the thrill of passion flowing
in the bed I choose to lay.

Rejection in my mind
of things that wound the soul
for kindness is the fuel
that sooths and makes us whole.

I remember as a child
summer days so wild and free
innocence was my religion
am I now – not me

Childhood ends, when we begin
to chain our hearts with grief
acceptance is the trigger
for peace and true relief.

"To have good memories is to live twice"

ENEMIES   (I wrote this after watching a demonstration in
            London 2009 on the sad Arab Israeli conflict)

Hearts bleed, terrified flesh
beseeching, Middle East's tombs
soaked in blood, sad prayers
despair from mothers' wombs.

Compassion vanished
kindness dead
children's minds changed
revenge now fed.

Poisonous history
trapping mankind
enemies from birth
leaderships blind.

Stop this madness
cease this killing
halt this cruelty
but, they are not willing.

"No man is my enemy who never wronged me"

OLDER

Nothing prepares our mind
when years become unkind.

Lines on our face reveal
our beauty time did steal.

Youth has past, conceal our age
lie to ourselves, shake with rage.

Waste not one day
till we're old and grey.

Live in dreams awake
memories are not fake.

Look back not in sorrow
from pleasures storehouse borrow.

For sudden violent death
could guillotine our breath.

Any moment of any day
life's vital lesson: live TODAY.

So seal the deal
to your heart reveal.

Commit not the crime
of not valuing time.

"The older my mind grows the younger my heart sows .... love"

DESTRUCTION   *(This poem was published in a Tallaght magazine, Dublin)*

Selfishness in my heart
was the bullet that tore apart
two lives welded into one.

And if wisdom was for sale
true love would never fail
nor bullets leave that gun.

Leave they did
blood was shed
two hearts
cried bitter tears.

Gone forever
like melted snow
love's dreams
down the years.

"To destroy the thing we love is like skating on very thin ice"

THE POVERTY OF RICHES

It cannot buy one true friend
and it never could buy trust
it knows not how the heart to mend
when money turns to dust.

Family is true treasure
with laughter at the table
simple things bring pleasure
the fool has bought the fable.

Riches are spent in giving
a paradox but true
when the giver of gifts starts living
each day dies born, anew.

Banks are filled with cash and gold
profits made in every city
useless when life grows old
priceless if bottom line is pity.

Deposits made in the bank of life
yield dividends beyond compare
time spent with children, friends and wife
breathes magic in the air.

It frees from ignorance and slavery
on dreams decisively now can act
conducts a mission of kindly bravery
wonderful asset, obvious fact.

"I would rather be rich than poor, like Andrew Carnegie; a doer"

REWARD   (I wrote this poem on our wonderful magical third anniversary 1973 before any of our six beautiful children had been born)

I saw her

I met her

We fell in love

We courted

Laughed

Learned

Cried

Grew

I married her

We slept together

In pain together

"Please hold my hand, it's our baby, I'm scared"

Then...

Blood water beauty life

Mine her's ours

Perfect beautiful reward

Of a simple love.

"My reward was her laughter"

LOVE IS BORN

Out of the blue
my beating heart knew.
Blood in my flesh
feelings so fresh.

I just knew
it was you.
No words were said
as I was led
to plan a life
with you my wife
but did she suspect
my deep respect.

A mystery shorn
my dream reborn
today I live
my past forgive.

"Born twice"

THE LOVER'S FACE

Five inches by three
the human face.
Like snowdrops
Intricate
Different
Beautiful.

But oh!
The Lover's Face
It's glow
Smile
Radiance
Beauty
Dancing eyes.

The look
That special look
Reserved for love
For romance
For her lover
His lover
Alone
Each one
More beautiful
Than
Miss Mona Lisa.

"Hair, skin, eyes, teeth, four colours on a lover's face: Loving words spoken from the mouth, pinnacle of our tender race"

DEATH OF LOVE

Unimaginable
Unthinkable
Impossible
Yet
Tragically true.

To lose a lover
The one
Loved
Totally
Passionately
Forever.

How?
Why?
When?
What?

No, no, no!
Yes
Suddenly
Slowly
Silently
Dreams died
Love vanished
Feelings changed.

The pain
Shock
No future
No present
Daily grind.

Warmth to ice
Laughter to anger
Hope to despair
Friendship to enmity
Lover to stranger
Life to death
Victor to vanquished
Certainty to confusion.

Let go
No
Why?
I can't
You must.

O' the sweet, sweet
memories.

I want it again
I have learned
No more mistakes
Selfish pursuits
No more love funerals.

"The funeral of love is the burial of dreams"

I WONDER

Is she happy, is she free
is it possible she could bond to me.
I WONDER

Who has touched her heart before
does she know she has touched my core?
I WONDER

Why I let her slip away
what can I say to make her stay.
I WONDER

About her pain in the past
her future with joy, may it last.
I WONDER

How destiny strikes out of the blue
so to our dreams we must be true.
I WONDER

What is it she wants in a mate
if I try, am I too late.
I WONDER

What is this magic that ignites its spark
to kiss and cuddle, hold hands in the park.
I WONDER

Why once again Venus met Mars
is our future in the stars.
I WONDER

Will she give me a second chance
to capture again a great romance.
I WONDER

Can she see how very much
her tender heart I want to touch.
I WONDER

"I wonder does she wonder"

HARVEST

Women look at men with interest
men look at them with lust
the dynamic here is wounded
corrosive dangerous rust.

Men's eyes visualise pleasure
women's hearts hold what is real
yet each man kills the thing he loves
for broken hearts do not heal.

What is this thing called love
some win it till the day they die
others squander and abuse it
the worst fool of all, will lie.

Youth is aging innocence
forged in the furnace of life
unaccustomed to disappointments
fate awaits razor and knife.

Love is the food we all crave
its medicine like music does heal
many wounded hearts and lives
for loves charter is in its seal.

To have loved and lost is life
and nothing can ease that pain
the wisest of men will learn
and if lucky, find love again.

Hold fast to dreams, for if dreams live
in receptive hearts, that might forgive
sickening wrongs and egregious acts
for most of life's dramas, are more than dry facts.

"We reap what we grow"

SUNDAYS

I love Sunday mornings
all day long I'm free
from working hard all week
now, I can be me.

Stay in bed read the papers
this is the way to live
if only more days were like Sunday
There is nothing I would not give.

Time to listen to children's problems
a joy to watch them play
I believe the concept of a Sabbath
I need this lazy day.

For 24 hours I can do
anything at all I choose
go for a jog, clean the yard
have a beer, watch the news.

The highlight of this day
is something simple yet so fine
sitting down with family
Sunday dinner enjoying wine.

Phones do not ring
people do not call,
for to disturb a man on Sunday
is really off the wall.

Night time comes, off to bed
refreshed, relaxed, serene,
ready to face Monday morning,
a contented human being.

"If food, sleep and wine are medicine, then a day of rest is all three"

INSTABILITY   *(Internet damage)*

The raging currents of
Information overload
Confuse amuse educate and shock
Too much too soon too fast
Stop, and definitely block.

Anchor's unhooked
Drifting unhinged
Plans unchained
Dreams spoiled
Days unchecked
Words unspoken.

Computer commandoes attack
Time peace purpose
Pleasure sleep mind.

Do this, do that, do nothing
Do everything at once
We are Edvard Munch's "Scream"
Contentment blind.

Facebook Base-book Race-book
Thief of time
Communication originator
Living screen
Real time.

"The thieving of time is the internet's crime"

MY HOME

Do I imagine it, or is it true
this place where I rest my feet
a little paradise of peace I call
my home, at the end of our street.

Sure it needs this and it needs that
there's always something to be done
but no matter how much I do
I have still only just begun.

Nevertheless, when I go home
and switch on the T.V
I can forget my day
relax and truly be me.

The kids may shout
I don't really mind
because I'm in my castle
this is what I find.

I'm safe at home, it's where I belong
I can totally unwind and relax
enjoy the bustle and noise in each room
who cares if the walls have cracks.

When friends call, or children's pals arrive
we always invite them in
for not to do so, is quite unpardonable
and in a child's mind, a sin.

I sometimes think, why not move
buy a house that is bigger and better
then my heart grows faint as I realise
a happy home is like a friend's letter

nice to get, a joy to read
there's nothing more I need.

No matter how tough life gets
with all its woes and knocks
I never roam far from my little snug
built with wood and a few stone blocks.

It's not the building or its size
or its lovely view out at the sky
it's the place where I have chosen to live
happily, probably, till the day I die.

"East, west, home is best"

BROKEN DREAMS

The ties that bind
are pure and blind
harness our new friends
but pals are few
when life is blue
tragic when friendship ends.

We never mean to hurt
those whom we respect
but we do, and do it often
when we are guilty of neglect.

Life's pressures its true, are many
and they take up our time
but friendship is a rare pearl
and to ignore it, is a crime.

We are spendthrifts of what's precious
if we allow friends drift away
and the tide of time won't wait
as each one goes their way.

There are some things necessary
as we search for happiness
family, friends and purpose
not much more, but nothing less.

All of us regret
some dreams that did go sour
but this is life without a wife
and must not turn us dour.

Broken dreams and shattered schemes
make not a man of clay
for I rise and realise
new dreams begin, today.

*"There are millions who awake from broken dreams and sleep
contentedly in the arms of an exciting new one"*

LIFE OF BIRTH

Each birth on this planet
results from an act of will
often-times born from love
yet sometimes violence still.

Her body yields for that splash
of sperm rushing to the womb
the clock of life starts ticking
and ends in a silent tomb.

One maniac succeeds
in the goal to fertilise
as her stomach grows, she knows
captured is life's golden prize.

Millions died so one could live
that is the reality of fate
regardless of the struggle
they simply were too late.

In time she knows, two months gone
prepares for the other seven
thirty more weeks and she seeks
knowledge to prepare for heaven.

She talks to dad and he's glad
but it's mother who must be there
when she opens her legs as she begs
"ease the pain please, it's only fair."

Months pass by and feelings deepen
her baby she loves with a passion
knows in her heart, till the day she dies
new life, is no passing idle fashion.

Eyes glisten for her lover
who gave this gift of life
thinking in her quiet moments
'I now am fulfilled, as wife.'

Boy or girl, does not matter
so long as it has good health
if that comes true, we realise
this surely, is true wealth.

Pregnancy has changed her
in every single way
days consumed with longing
for that special exciting day.

She lies there pushing
her baby finally born
gasping through misty eyes
now gone is the painful thorn.

To bring forth such wondrous joy
a woman has to bleed
and as love explodes in ecstasy
a man must give his seed.

She feeds her baby from warm soft breasts
as she contentedly gives vital milk
then she cleans and gazes on her child
of flesh and bone and silk.

All scientists who have ever lived
cannot create one single eye
philosophers who have wondered
cannot answer, why?

Musicians and poets worldwide agree
on one fundamental they are sure
love and life all begin
in a babies heart so pure.

"All questions about life's purpose can be summed up by watching a baby being born, and listening to it cry"

THE HOUSE OF LOVE   *(Ode to a very sick little girl)*

I sometimes wonder, if there's a God above
but not when I visit Saibhe's house of love,
for living within these walls of stone
is a beautiful little girl, who is never alone.

Painted on walls are beanstalks and flowers
music makes her smile a precious few hours,
candles lighting that quiver and glow
and if Saibhe could speak, she would want us to know.

Yes I am sick and not really well
if you look at my face this you can tell,
I see with my heart and not with my eyes
and when loving hands hold me they ease my cries.

Wonderful nurses come every day
they tell me stories like 'Jack and Gill'
polish my nails, fix my hair
and love me more, because I'm ill.

I also have three amazing sisters
Natalie, Dionne and Sofia,
when they come and talk to me
their voices sound like, Ave Maria.

Lola Bell has arrived
brought us much joy
we needed some laughter
I'm glad she's not a boy.

Let me tell everyone here today
listen carefully to what I say
I have a great Grandma, her name is Ann
whom I cherish, would do anything I can
if I was not sick, to show her I care
but I can't as I'm strapped in this metal chair.

For four months she visited me every day
she would cuddle and hold me and beside me lay
for she is my flesh
she is my blood
she feels my pain
is there anyone so good?

Today Saibhe is seven
and she joined Jesus's fold
she made her communion
we should copy her mould.

Her mam and dad
love her very much
and when she is crying
she calms at their touch.

But let Saibhe speak
about her father and mother
a gift from God
she would have no other.

My dad is real cool
he's so full of love
and if I could kneel down
I would thank God above.

For this man of steel
with power in his heart
who loves me every day
and would never depart.

He works and he prays
that I might get well
yes I live in his house
but it's in his heart that I dwell.

Now I come to my daily rock
my wonderful mother got a terrible shock
the day I was born
when she almost died
when shown my photo
she laughed and then cried.

For here was her baby
who needed much love
and through oceans of tears
asked her strange God above.

Why is little Saibhe sick?
she did nothing wrong
please give me the strength
to make her belong.

She makes me laugh
she holds me tight
I simply love her
with all my might.

This poem is a story
reflecting the dignity of life
about a man and his family
a sick child and his wife.

How through tenderness and tears
worry and power
a family bonded
to this very hour.

They look to the future
that no-one can tell
and pray with one voice
sweet Saibhe, please get well.

"The joy of a sick child's smile, sometimes makes it all worthwhile"

THE END

As I edge towards oblivion

and contemplate my grave

the meaningless echo of nothingness

leaves me awfully sad not brave.

"The end shall one day be our beginning, if there is a God"

GIFT OF LOVE

Two lives
One spirit
Two hearts
Three words
I love you

Love gives
Love lives
Love grows
Love shows

Love's lift
Love's gift
Love shares
Love bares

Love feels
Love kneels
Love succeeds
Love breeds

Love's power
Love's shower
Life's goal
Love's foal

Life without love is like
Bones without flesh
Wombs without babies
Days without purpose
Nights without joy
Flowers without water

To give love
is to make the giver
Godlike

King of love
Queen of love
Conqueror
Inspirer

To receive love
makes us feel:
Alive
Aglow
Thrilled
Reborn
Ecstatic
Hopeful
Fulfilled
Happy

Of all life's gifts
none
equals love.

"To know love is to know yourself"

DISASTER   *(On the recession)*

Ireland weeps
for her past
Security lost
Meaning gone
Financial instability
Credibility weakened
Future uncertain
Banks lied
Some died
Easy credit
Hard lessons
Tears of innocence
Mothers wave children away
Fathers cry
It's over
Aftershock
Lost trust
Reality found
Laughter through tears
Anguish
Pain
A nation buckled
Lost
Confused
Blind
Debt
Despair
Loans rejected
Overdrafts over

Fiscal fission
IMF
ECB
Stress
Cutbacks
Loss
More worry
Optimism damaged

"Recession teaches us a fact of life, nothing is guaranteed"

WORDS   *(Written in Boston USA 2013)*

Of all the words
fed into our head
some are dangerous
others leave us bled.

Perhaps the most blinding
"let there be light"
as darkness descended
to savage delight.

Unleashed on man
his selfish heart
jealousy and war
commenced its start.

Innocence destroyed
paradise lost
graveyards hungry
armies deployed.

Religions invented
to soothe the soul
spells and priests
man's god, false ghoul.

Philosophers searched
for wisdom and gold
as children died young
and minds grew old.

Here on earth
was bad with good
sickness and health
poisonous blood.

"We declare war"
became mankind's creed
as vengeance crippled
the young with its seed.

"Words are permanent
and cannot be unsaid,
and words that wound the heart
leave love and friendship dead"

SEVENTY

The day I was born
my mother said, 'He is perfect'
I am not, she was
because to a child a loving mother is
just because.

The day I was five
I felt so alive
loved by mam and dad
I now had sisters
this made me glad.

The day I was ten
I wondered when
I too could be a man
we played on the street
in our bare feet
got into trouble and ran.

The day I was fifteen
I kissed my princess
went to the beach and swam
worked and played, I was made
For once I knew, who I am.

The day I was twenty
Life was good, fights and blood
few regrets, none to mention
little did I know, time would grow
and soon, too soon, my pension.

The day I was twenty-five
Marriage came knocking on my door
being in love, thanked God above

and wanted, truly wanted
nothing more.

The day I was thirty
two beautiful daughters
made my life complete
family united in daily joy
could anything be more sweet.

The day I was thirty five
I felt so very alive
now had a son, lots of fun
the future beyond, so bright
well let's get real, sometimes its shite.

The day I was forty
Our youngest about to arrive
the baby, sometimes a lady
now the family was eight
they laughed and played
and when I prayed
the only word needed was great.

The day I was forty five
I knew this May was now halfway
and time was going too fast
friends had died, families cried
I wondered, does anything last?

The day I was fifty
To be honest
I was really quite shocked
so I went into town
and simply got locked.

The day I was fifty five
I was getting 'old'
wrinkles on my face
our doctor, my ace
in summer, feeling cold.

The day I was sixty
Awh Jaysus
the shock, was beyond belief
cannot be true, it makes me blue
and medicine now brings relief.

The day I was sixty five
Holy fuck, just my luck
but I shall never complain
I'll laugh and sing, dance and prance
knowing life is laughter and pain.

The day I turned seventy
It's no joke, I'm still the same bloke
and I love my family and friends
grandchildren adore, please give me some more
well, that really all depends!

So if there is any advice
that can make life more nice
it has to be forgiveness and love
as I sit here tonight
it feels just right
to look up and thank God above.

"Life is too short to not love, and too long to not have found it"

WILL YOU MARRY ME

I never thought I would want
to leave my home
but I left the womb.

I never believed I could leave
my brothers and sisters
but sometimes left them cold.

I never imagined
I might leave
my country
but I rarely voted.

I never conceived
leaving my friends
but on holiday rarely sent cards.

Then
one of life's amazing questions arrived
will you marry me?

Shock
Thrill
Joy
Bliss
Wonder
Fear
Happiness.

The dawning that dreams
can come true.

Suddenly
all things I held sacred
I was willing to abandon
as Shakespeare confirmed in;
'The Two Gentlemen of Verona'

Leave
Say goodbye
For love (not for marriage)
For love
Love-love-love.

Will you marry me?
Yes
I want to be with you, forever
And I with you
Will we have children
Yes
Never change (a game changer for many)
I won't
I love you
And I you.

And so it goes
Generation after generation
Few of us learning
Oh yes, hearing
But rarely learning
From others mistakes.

"Will you marry me?" is a question everyone in love should ask"

MY TOWN *(Ode to a great city Dublin)*

I was born in Dublin city
thirty five years ago
loved time on its streets
sunshine, rain or snow.

There's something special about my town
I can say that from my heart
so many good things to boast about
I don't know where to start.

I'll begin with my estate
happy days spent as a child
quiet as a mouse
in my mansion of a house
once I hit the streets, went wild.

School in Inchicore
walks in Phoenix Park
chestnut fights in autumn
life was all a lark.

Growing up in Dublin
would not be complete
if someone did not take you
for a stroll up O'Connell street.

Bewleys for tea or coffee
Grafton Street for style
Moore Street for its dealers
Dublin Zoo for a smile.

The beauty of Stephen's Green
when the Corpo organised a band
ducks swimming, children playing
we had our free Disneyland.

Beshoffs for fish and chips
your local to sink the black
every weekend in Dublin
there was music and the craic.

Bells on Sunday morning
reminding of the night before
worshipping childhood gods
with headaches oh so sore.

Like many sons and daughters
I experienced sad exile
but on arrival home
my blood would sometimes boil.

At the difference in my city
everything changed so fast
as I grew up in innocence
I thought my town would last.

But nothing stays the same
I should have seen the power
of a city fighting for its life
and seizing its finest hour.

The Millennium had arrived
our Dublin stood erect
visitors from round the world
came and paid respect.

To a capital that equals any
in four corners of the globe
one felt pride in the Mansion House
our Lord Mayor in his robe.

Not everything is rosy
I know it never was
it's easy to complain
see our city's flaws.

Crime has increased
fear has raised its head
many are now afraid
when it's time to go to bed.

But if it's any consolation
there are other towns much worse
where to walk down the street
you could lose more than your purse.

So I accept my city
with its good and bad
and I love it even more
then when I was a lad.

The sea is on the east
rich farmland to its west
Lovely Howth to the north
Bray in the south, we're blessed.

To live in Dublin town
having everything so near
it's no wonder that we Dubliners
are filled with memories dear.

This is my eternal city
full of familiar places
but its most important asset
are its people's smiling faces.

The buildings are important
with much history off renown
oh yes my friends, I say again
Dublin is my town.

"I am so proud to call Dublin my home"

FIRST

The first to apologise
is the bravest.

The first to forgive
is the strongest.

The first to forget
is the happiest.

(Author unknown)

"I would rather be last at anything, if it meant losing my friend who was first"

WHY

What are our lives
we live and die
refuse to know
truth of why.

Why of life
hate of death
how of truth
our last breath.

Because of love
we dig for meaning
because of that
no more scheming.

Who really knows
why?
why?
why we live?

Existential madness
is anything real?
We lose our dreams
we find our questions.

Is anything genuine?
is it me
to live
to love
to question

to hold
family, oh yes family
that is the answer.

"If a child asks; why? dozens of times every day, why do adults stop asking the one word in any language that demands an honest answer? Why?

FIRE

Life is a raging burning fire

Don't add to it with spite and ire

Love is the only thing that saves

Down broken years till our cold graves.

"I would rather burn with love, than freeze with hate"

DISCOVERY   *(Written on my return from London in 1963 when I was seventeen)*

When I was young I went far away
I know not why my heart went astray
I left a good home and parents to be proud
I don't understand, why I followed the crowd.

for seventeen years I wandered alone
for all that time my heart was at home
one day I thought, why am I here?
why not go home? there is nothing to fear
my parents will welcome me, they shall be glad
why in the first place, did I make them so sad.

The journey began with my heart beating wild
back to the place I knew as a child
at last I arrived at the town of my birth
why did I wander from this heaven on earth?

My father looked old, my mother looked tired
when my eyes met theirs I just cried and cried
at last I am happy
no more will I cry
for here I will stay
and here I will die.

"When I realised I was the prodigal son I discovered the depth of my parents love"

LIFE GOES ON   *(Wrote this when I was eighteen)*

A child is born what raving joy
a man and woman produced a boy,
the supreme moment of any man's life
a child burst forth, from his loving wife.

Silent prayers to a God from his heart
life so wonderful, why must it depart?
ears, nose, legs, absolute perfection
innocence, purity, deep reflection.

All babies are equal when first naked born
hearts and minds not yet been torn.
My first tender years were carefree spent
the following few somehow just went.

School came and learning of laws
bittersweet, wait! life has its clause,
those childhood days of fun and tears
soon disappeared with mad rushing years,
suddenly you blossom, suddenly you bloom
OK Mr. Earth, for me make room.

Exciting days were those young teens
days filled with yearning, days filled with dreams,
young manhood, young womanhood one day arrive
you're proud, you're happy magnificently alive.

Challenges, disappointments, all part of the game
from mans beginning it has been the same,
with adulthood comes problems and achievements so rare
you strive and you drive, till your hopes you lay bare.

Next comes acceptance of what is you
years roll by, nothing new...
Old age comes, an uninvited guest
never leaves till it puts you to rest.

It's hard to believe I am old and grey
this feeble body knows I've had my day,
mind wanders back to lost glorious youth
I loved it, miss it, yes that's the truth.

If only once again I could be a healthy young man
fulfil that wish, I would give you all I can,
but I am grateful and thankful I have lived so long
goodbye sweet life, to mother earth I belong.

"Sweet bloom of youth squandered in pleasure, this is the truth and that was our treasure"

A WOODEN BOX

Each coffin I see
lowered in cold clay,
I decide
more family, friends and play.

For who knows
the hour of our demise,
then, no more music
dancing or sunrise.

What is complex man
but an existential mystery,
causing waterfalls of tears
down our blood drenched history.

Each coffin I see
sinking in the ground,
I ask why?
Why am I unbound?

From women I've loved
friends I have lost,
is it maybe on my heart
there is some freezing frost.

Each coffin I see
buried in a hole,
I swear to execute
my lifelong noble goal.

To practice kindness
that is free to give,
brings joy to hearts
as we truly live.

"It's not the number of breaths we take that matters, it's the number that take our breath away"

COMPLICATED SIMPLICITY   *(I wrote this as a younger man)*

God's highest creation, man
His most beautiful, woman
together produce love, life, loyalty and
all emotion that embellishes our human spirit.

One man, one woman
Two lives entangled
Forever caressing
Forever seeking
Forever hoping
Happiness for each other.

Two lives crashed together
Female and male
Young and innocent
Happy and hoping
Embarrassed and brash
Laughed and cried
Learned together
The penalty true love imposes.

"Loyalty for life"
cried Eros, the god of love,
"Oh yes" replied the owners of something beautiful
the novices of loves inception.

Years exposes actors
Time is friend and enemy
to those claiming unyielding loyalty.

Thousands of hours swiftly passed
hundreds of moments lavished
our lovers with unforgettable
total happenings of love
in its cherished frailty
precious, perfect, to blaze
between two hearts into eternity.

Two became one absolutely
in desire, in gladness, in anger, in reconciliation
until one felt the thoughts, heart, pain
and greatness of the other self.

Years mangled, scarred
yes relentlessly crucified the outward flesh
smashed the body, wrecked the strength
slowed the speed, mocked noble efforts of the mind
yes, but the spirit of love triumphed.

"Innocence is like virginity, once gone, gone forever"

LOVE   *(Wrote this when I was 16)*

Difficult quality to explain
Why?
Exciting to chase
Exhilarating to conquer
Execrable to lose.

Tricks the heart
Scares the mind
Upsets the nerves
Shatters style
Wonderful!

Smell the grass
Sing a new song
Walk faster
Sleep smiling
Feel the earth
Lick that breeze
Possessed!

Masculine
Feminine
In love, tender
Tender is the night.

"Of all the words ever written, sung or spoken about love, none gives more hope than; God is love"

THE FINAL WISH   *(On 'The Troubles' wrote in 1971)*

Fighting subsides
Words begin
Excitable tempers simmer
Drunks get drunk
Jokers joke
Women laugh
Children scream.

Time marches one way
On and gone
Religion equals opposite thoughts
Therefore hate, violence, failure
The gods of sex, money, nationalism laugh
Mock the gods of Ireland old
Land produces food, health, nature
In its ugly beauty.

Gifts as such don't stop with a border
Fifty years later arguments continue
Father tells son
Son tells son
Hearts harden
Visions disappear
New ones created
Fighting continues.

Help!
Ireland is dying
In its struggle to be born
The world is puzzled

Holy Ireland
Unholy rebellion 1971.

Our past is blood
The present, tears
Future ashes
Irelands malignant cancer
Hate
Irelands delicate cure
love
Idealistic is the dream
There is no other solution.

Minds enslaved to tradition
Right or wrong
People live
And die
Love and laugh.

Political dreams
Come and go
Elusive solution
LOVE.

"We have enough religion to make us hate, but not enough to make us love one another"
- Jonathan Swift.

TRUTH   *(Wrote this when I was about 16 years of age)*

There is a word
much spoken about
a word that is used
through life in and out.

It cuts and it hurts
that is quite true
a word that is practiced
by people too few.

It's not that they
are afraid of truth
but just that they use it
anytime it might suit.

What truly amazes
about this part off speech
is that peoples own children
they sometimes don't teach.

It is ignored and twisted
every day to suit man
he will abuse and avoid it
anyway that he can.

It is said that truth
"will set you free"
but for man this proverb
might well as not be.

Not all men are liars
some are quite truthful
these men enjoy life
for them it is fruitful.

"If truth sets us free as the young Rabbi said, then why are millions trapped in prisons called conflict"

TIRED   *(I wrote this at about 16 years of age)*

When I look at the world
I take a deep sigh
When I study mankind
I just want to cry.

So much anger
So much hate
Where is the love
That was of late?

Man could be free
Of most of his pain
If leaders would say
"Let us be sane."

I don't think it will be
That every nation
Shall stop their mad race
For world domination.

For man in his pride
And self styled elation
Shall refuse to destroy
His own wicked creation.

Then who will suffer?
Yes the whole human race
Only then shall man cry
For Gods protection and grace.

Man's inhumanity to man
Just what can I say!
Only one thing
It will happen one day.

There is too much crime
too much tribulation
"oh what shall become
Of Gods brilliant creation."

It is said that death
Is the supreme peace
Instead it should be
The gift of release.

"If history is a great teacher, why are we blind to its disasters? And condemned to repeat its madness"

CHEATED   *(I wrote this at 16 years of age in relation to the Cuban Missile Crisis in 1962)*

It is strange that generals
in all their splendour,
should dictate to their men
never surrender.

Protect your country
die for your land,
but is it not true
they kill with their hand.

They brainwash the mass
destroy people's minds,
oh what can be done
to show them its lies.

There is too much corruption
and too much hypocrisy,
from men who profess
prominent democracy

So soldiers obey
and go out to battle,
to do or to die
then treated like cattle.

So people wake up
be you not led wrong,
by men who say
we are quite strong.

Find out the truth
question your teaching,
thereafter immune
from diabolical preaching.

"War is the ugliest expression of man's corruption"

TRUTH WILL TRIUMPH   *(Wrote in San Francisco - 1970)*

Thrill to truth
Rewarding is truth
Understanding is truth
Today truth
Hope in truth.

Write truth
Impressive is truth
Live truth
Love truth.

Trust in truth
Respect truth
Immortal is truth
Unending truth
Marry truth
Priceless is truth
Happiness from truth.

"I would rather tell a lie than reveal a truth that caused the death of one innocent person"

IS IT ANY WONDER

With
Broken dreams
Impossible schemes
Is it any wonder

People
Become terribly shy
And others sly
Is it any wonder

Look
Friends so rare
Does anyone care
Is it any wonder

And
Struggles of life
Cut like a knife
Is it any wonder

Some
Friends lie
Others die
Is it any wonder

With
Disaster and madness
Betrayal and badness
Is it any wonder

Millions
Wish to get high
Regret and then sigh
Is it any wonder

Yes
Sickness and death
Until our last breath
Is it any wonder

Then
Guilt and shame
Our first words are blame
Is it any wonder

"I wonder at the wonder of life"

LOST

I was not looking
when I found her.

She was not lost
when I lost her.

It was I who lost my mind
searching for lost treasure.

Although I was totally blind
it was I who was selfish.

"Anything lost might be found, except two things: Time and a soulmate"

BEWARE

Who knows the reasons

why we stray!

Who can explain

why we play!

In others people's gardens

to sow our seeds

but what erupts

are poisonous weeds.

"To stray is like a wasp's sting to the heart - Beware"

THE CAT

Incessant scratching slowly woke me
as I lay in silence on my bed,
it was the middle of night's darkness
when it dawned, I was not dead.

I open my eyes and hear the cries
of a wailing cat and distant bell,
and wonder in the dark of silence
is this another night of hell.

As I lay in my room amidst the gloom
memories of yore return,
the joy of being young is always sung
for its youth that we truly burn.

Tick, tock, beats the bedroom clock
a gift from my mother long dead,
its rhythmic sound is all around
comforts me as I lie in my bed.

Scratch, scratch, scratch
Oh my god, he's at the latch,
is this the deadly reaper
who wants a frightened sleeper?
I feel the need to cry
oh no, am I going to die?

Scratch, scratch, scratch
and then an awful screech,
I almost fainted with the shock

who is this monster trying to reach
I'm so glad I turned that lock.

My commitment to a god ignited
its fuse was lit by fear,
I prayed to Rome's Clementia
have mercy on this phony seer.

An angry cat has an awful scream
some say, it has nine lives,
but I'm the cat that got the cream
for I have had nine wives.

It's only a cat on my front mat
I now can return to sleep,
my dreams to keep, as I sleep deep
for tonight; I shall not weep.

"I cannot think of a good quote for a bad cat nor can I think of a bad quote for a good cat"

THE SEVEN DEADLY WINS

To win the love of a good woman or man

To win good health

To win respect from family

To win loyal friends

To win peace of mind

To win contentment

To win a noble, humble, kind heart.

"To win all seven of the above is to lose ourselves to love"

WHEN I AM BEING LOVED

Heart thunders to dance

Mind frozen in time

Spirit alive to music

Soul rests in joy

Dreams fulfilled

Life a Greek Chorus

Goal for lasting magic

Anxiety vanished

Hate disappeared

Love - my being

Now and forever.

"Love is oxygen for hearts"

WHO ARE WE

Who am I
Am I me like you are thee
The question is existential.
I wonder why, I sometimes cry
and keep things confidential.

Am I real
This pain I feel
for wars that plague mankind,
children cry, hearts do sigh
peace melts from my mind.

Is this me
That people see
on first impressions judge,
for no one knows our highs and lows
and to reveal ourselves we fudge.

Who are we
Are we governed by our passions
Do we truly know our mind
The answer is irrelevant
If we are always humbly kind.

The Greeks put 'Know Thyself' on the Temple of Apollo the god of music, healing and poetry. However; 'Ama te ipsum' is Latin for 'Love yourself' which is far simpler and therefore much better

LOOKING

I looked for knowledge
and found wisdom.

I looked for nothing
and found love.

I looked for purpose
and found kindness.

I looked for fulfilment
and found you.

"When we find purpose; we stop looking"

HYPOCRISY

Christians preach love

some practice hate.

Many are kind

but willingly blind

to biblical malice

as priests raise the chalice

some elders grin

when followers sin

by being cruel

then adding fuel

from written precepts

by quoting concepts

alien to the young rabbi.

he said:

"To love others the way we would like to be loved"

Therefore if I follow him

I should love my fellowman

that is, if I can.

Jesus commanded us to love God and our neighbour, surely, an
invitation is preferable than an injunction.
N.B. I am not a Christian but then neither was he.

FIVE MEN

Oscar said:
"The older we get the more difficult it is to make new friends"
He was both wrong and right.

Five mature men
Not really 'knowing' each other
Met in Northern Spain
Summer of 2018.

Spent eight days together
Ate, drank
Walked and talked.

On the third day
The poet said;
"Lads we're having a good time
but our conversation is mundane,
so why don't we tell each other in one minute
the happiest day of our lives
and the second minute
the saddest day of our life."

The clown said:
"That's a great idea"

The consigliere said:
"Yes, but we must be honest"

The joker said (in innocence)
"Ha ha, this is funny"

The wise man said;
"Since we are all older men
this could be dangerous"

The poet spoke first:
"The happiest day of my life was
the day I married my beautiful wife
and
the saddest day of my life was
22 happy years later, we got divorced."

In reply,
the wise man spoke one word;
"Why?"
The poet replied with two words:
" My selfishness"

There was an awkward silence
and someone said:
"Next"

The consigliere spoke solemnly:
"The happiest day of my life was,
when I loved a wonderful woman neighbour and
one Valentines day I put a flower pot and a card at her door.
We touched fingers through her letter box
childish and innocent, but true,
that was one of the happiest days of my life."

"The saddest day of my life was,
I was about six years old
and I heard my father and mother argue loudly.
I then heard words come from my mother

that traumatised me ever since,
they were shocking, terrifying, unbelievable words;
'I am leaving this house'
that, was the saddest day of my life."

We all stood in frozen silence.
Then

The wise guy gave his happiest and saddest days in reverse:
"The saddest day of my life was
the day I married a woman I did not love.
I did it because I got her pregnant
but it gets worse
we had two beautiful children I adored
and after eight years I left.

The day I left my heart was breaking
as I took my last look into our kitchen
it was lashing rain
my two children stood there with their mother
who loved them too
while I stood outside in the cold rain
crying my eyes out."

"The most joyful day of my life was,
the moment I knew
the new woman in my life whom I loved
loved me too.
So now I have my two children who love me
and a good woman who adores me."

We stood mesmerized.
The joker spoke:

"The happiest day of my life was,
The day I got married
I was nervous, extremely nervous
but felt like I was walking on air.
I thought life doesn't get much better than this
but it did, with the magnificent birth of my first born child."

"And my saddest day,
bereavement.
I cannot cope with the deaths of those I love
so I have had some very bad days in my life
especially the deaths of my mother and father."

There was silence in the room.

Then finally the clown spoke:
"The happiest day of my life was,
the day I married.
I was ecstatically happy
but the only problem with that was
I was a child-boy
with all the future problems that implies."

"And the saddest day of my life was,
when I watched my loving wife cry
and through her sobs she uttered five words
which devastated my clown's world"
'I don't love you anymore.'"

The rest of our holiday was more revealing.

"To share joy and sorrow is from friends borrow, wisdom and pain
which keeps a man sane"

HONEST OPINION

He expressed his honest opinion
believing it to be true,
told it with conviction
for this he ignorantly knew.

He would not entertain
or listen to contradictions,
hated educated logic
preferring childhood fictions.

*"All opinions are suspect until indisputable evidence is produced, it
is then that those who love truth are revealed"*

(The following six poems were published in my second book titled ANY BODY CAN LOSE WEIGHT - EXCEPT YOU)

THE MIRROR

Our face reveals true age
Hearts reveal sweet youth
Tears reveal our woes
Words reveal our truth.

Actions reveal our nature
Habits reveal our schemes
Vision reveals our minds
Goals reveal our dreams.

Lies reveal our cunning
Purpose reveals our life
Joy reveals acceptance
Death, cuts like a knife.

Thoughts reveal the person
Eyes reveal the soul
Plans reveal our values
Spirituality makes us whole.

Love reveals our being
Sex reveals our core
Passion reveals nobility
Life calls out for more.

Friends reveal personality
Enemies reveal our past
Family reveal our genes
Children born to last.

A face reveals our book
Expressions reveal our prose
Laughter reveals our music
And love is our red rose.

*My mother said to me, "John, when I look in the mirror and see
wrinkles on my face I know there are none on my heart"*

FLESH

I eat too much
and walk too little
that is why I'm fat,
but you're not at
where I am sat
with feelings
oh so brittle.

I want to lose
cut down on booze
I need to make that choice,
but it's not nice
to cut out vice
or listen
to my inner voice.

I shall decide
for I have pride
that decision I now choose,
and I shall burn
no stone unturn
those lousy pounds to lose.

**"I am not just blood, bone and flesh, I have a mind and this is the
instrument that can break every single addiction"**

FRIENDSHIP   **(Ode to my great friends)**

There's a miracle of friendship

that dwells within the heart

we don't know how it happens

or where it gets its start

but the magic that it brings you

always gives a special lift

and you realise that friendship

is life's most precious gift.

(Author unknown)

"To have one true friend in our one life is the one sure thing that one should be eternally grateful for"

DECISION

I feel no shame
for being weak
nor excuses do I invent
I blame no one
for my mistakes
when pleasure
was my intent.

I will pay the price
for my 'faux pas'
and rectify my weight
by dancing on my appetites
before it is too late.

"Because I am weak, it is my constant battles that make me strong"

SUCCESS

I shall succeed
even if I bleed
I will try
no matter cry.

Yes I will
sweat to spill
gritted teeth
days are sweet.

I might fail
faults to nail
in the end
life will mend.

Eyes on prize
now realise
body pure
aim secure.

I cannot fail
vice impail
a body slim
mine to win.

"A little foolishness now and then is relished by the wisest of men"

EVERY DAY

Some days we lose
and some we win
others are great
on some we sin.

Some are slow
others fast
some so good
wish they'd last.

Some nights magic
others we forget
sleep comes gently
nothing to regret.

Every day nearer
our ultimate ambition
weight lost forever
and a slim condition.

"Every single day I shall do something, no matter how small, to make a big difference to my dream"

QUIET THOUGHTS   *(Wrote these when I was about 16)*

ENSLAVED

Character assassination - convention

OPIUM

Religion – A money maker when all else fails

FACT

Death – the beginning of nothing (until the resurrection, if there is a God)

ART LIVES!

Art- an appreciation of meaning, because of object

"I cogitate on life, meditate on death and appreciate every single breath"

WISDOM

She was unkind to me

I did not reciprocate

For why should sweet warm love

Transform to bitter cold hate

MEDITATIONS ON LIFE

"A man is not old whose heart is bold"

"The greatest deceits lurk in men's hearts"

"Suspicion is like acid on love and jealousy its poison"

"I have been joyless but with friends and family never loveless"

"We can print a lie, speak a lie, even live a lie, but in the end truth will triumph"

"The depth of our jealousy at others success is a true barometer of our own inadequacies"
 (I wrote this at the Cannes Film Festival, May 2018)

"All soldiers as trained killers are to be pitied. Consider the destruction they cause in the name of their cause, which is opposed to the other side's cause"

"Happiness is like mercury, it can easily slip through our fingers"

"To the true cynic everything is false"

"The trouble with truth is, truth might be trouble,
  but the trouble with lies is, they are poison and double"

"Beware the woman with a kind heart but in her damaged mind lurks an ice cold siren"

"False allegations are like acid on a true reputation"

"A person who attacks friends, wounds their own heart and life"

"Those who say they know the future, know they don't"

"Time is the one thing I have time for"

"The Arts challenge and console us, lift our standards, deepen our thinking, enliven our days and inspire our lives"

"Freedom from a bad friend is good for the mind"

"There is your opinion, my opinion and the alleged correct opinion, however they are all right and ...... wrong"

"Curiosity is the seed of all discovery"

"Opinion is the lowest form of evidence in law"

"Living each day as if it were our last, introduces sadness, living each day as if it is our first, brings pleasure joy and madness"

"If believing is receiving, things that are not true, will you change and rearrange? If not, what says that of you"

"A lie is like a hand grenade ..... with the pin pulled out"

"Kindness is the seed of all lasting joy"

"Friendship is like a babies smile, given freely, nothing asked in return and heart warming"

"Bitterness is like a leaking cyanide tablet in the mouth, it will poison the heart and eventually kill it"

"My trinity is, music, kindness and dancing"

"If the trinity of music, kindness and dancing had been taught to mankind, instead of theological treacheries, we would have had no religions and almost paradise on earth"

"At six we stare in amazement and wonder looking at a butterfly, at sixty many don't even notice them, I wonder why?"

"Most humans are lonely, but some never suffer loneliness"

"I shall never stop fighting my weaknesses, for it is this that makes me strong"

"Religion is the vehicle that preaches love but practices hate, with a sanctified smile and certified texts" (particularly in wartime)

"When we are betrayed by a friend that person reveals their depth"

"The reason I lost her is because she was lost"

"To reflect deeply in the night-time is to possibly live wisely in the daytime"

"When you accept yourself, you reject hurtful views from others"

"Mans madness for war is only equalled by his passion for violence"

A Short Story

Kindness is priceless

And that is why

Our family was rich

When I was

A poor little boy.

THE END.